ISBN 978-0-332-73140-7
PIBN 11234167

master plan

GRAND TETON

NATIONAL PARK / WYOMING

GRAND TETON

NATIONAL PARK / WYOMING

MASTER PLAN

UNITED STATES DEPARTMENT OF THE INTERIOR / NATIONAL PARK SERVICE

MASTER PLAN

GRAND TETON

NATIONAL PARK / WYOMING

UNITED STATES DEPARTMENT OF THE INTERIOR / NATIONAL PARK SERVICE

CONTENTS

preface

The startling beauty of the jagged Teton Range, thrusting
abruptly above the flat expanse of Jackson Hole, has
inspired powerful and enduring emotional responses in
modern man for more than a century and a half.

For the trappers and mountain men, the peaks were
guiding beacons in an unmapped land; for a Nation
moving west, a barrier to be avoided; and for the early
settlers, a harsh wilderness to be tamed. For much of the
first half of the 20th century, the Tetons and their
foreground were the subject of bitter strife between
private and public interests, and, for many years, they
were a measure of a family's dedication to preserving
the Nation's natural beauty. Thus, here, in an area set aside
for the preservation and enjoyment of its remarkable
natural features, a microcosm of the American epic is
represented, exemplifying a Nation's evolving attitudes
toward the land.

Today and in the future, Grand Teton National Park can
be the setting for a diverse array of exhilarating and satisfying
personal experiences, and a place in which the American
people can learn to reach a genuinely harmonious relationship
with their natural environment. This master plan is the
conceptual document that establishes guidelines for management and use of Grand Teton National Park within the bounds
of existing legislative commitments. It is the product of
several years' work by an outstanding team of leading citizens,
park planners, and management personnel, with substantial
input from the public. The plan deals with the park's purposes,
its resource values, its relationship to the regional environs, and
the means by which its resources may best be managed to
serve its purposes in a regional context.

summary

Grand Teton National Park was established to protect and provide for the American people's enjoyment of a matchless array of scenic and scientific resources in association with some intriguing reminders of the human past. The park's "products" are the diverse forms of human pleasure and enlightenment that it can provide, without consumption of those resources. This master plan sets up a number of management initiatives by which these ends may be achieved:

> Hold overnight accommodations, visitor convenience facilities, and wilderness trail development at levels not exceeding those established in 1971.

> Strictly control the pollutants produced as a result of park use.

> Reduce the impact upon the park of intrusive structures, including residential and operational facilities.

> Provide new modes and paths of visitor access to park experiences, no less convenient than those provided in the past, but resulting in reduced impact upon park resources.

> Carry on a communications program that gives park visitors and neighbors the opportunity to understand park resources and opportunities, and to sense the profound environmental effects resulting from seemingly routine demands for convenience or entertainment.

> Actively participate in bringing Federal, State, local entities, and individuals together for the development and implementation of a regional plan in which each unit of the regional mosaic is put to its best use.

> Restore natural fire and insect regimes in the park without endangering human lives or valuable cultural features.

> Further reduce unnecessary human intrusion on the park by eventually reducing or eliminating the park's elk-control program; reducing the impact of fishermen upon aquatic resources; minimizing the influences of Jackson Hole airport; and reducing the unnatural influences of water-control activities.

We do not intend to forfeit any of what is unique about Grand Teton National Park in the interests of providing for uses or facilities that are inappropriate to it.

2

background

PURPOSE

Grand Teton was established as a unit of the National Park System to protect the scenic and gelogical values of the Teton Range and Jackson Hole, and to perpetuate the park's indigenous plant and animal life. The park will interpret these natural and scenic values, in association with the historical significance of the region, in a manner that preserves these resources for the benefit and pleasure of present and future generations.

MANAGEMENT CATEGORY

Grand Teton, by the provisions of its establishment act, is a natural area.

LEGISLATIVE BACKGROUND AND COMMITMENTS

Grand Teton is subject to a number of legislative and other commitments that permit certain activities not usually allowed in a national park.

Approximately 150 square miles of the most rugged and spectacular portions of the Teton Range were set aside because of their wilderness values as Grand Teton National Park on February 26, 1929. Fourteen years later, on March 15, 1943, historic Jackson Hole, an adjacent and integral part of

Grand Teton's scene and story, was established as a national monument by Presidential proclamation. Controversy raged for the next 7 years over the legality of this proclamation, however.

Eventually, the conflicting issues were resolved, and a new Grand Teton National Park, incorporating both the original park and the contested monument, was established by congressional action through Public Law 81-787 on September 14, 1950. This act repealed all other provisions of law specifically applicable to the former park and monument.

The following are portions of significant public laws and administrative actions that expressly commit park management to certain practices.

Legislative Provisions Under Public Law 81-787
These designated and opened rights-of-way, including stock driveways, over and across Federal lands within the exterior boundary of the park, for the movement of persons and property to and from national forests and State and private lands adjacent to the park.

Leases, permits, and licenses issued or authorized with respect to the Federal lands within the park and in effect on September 14, 1950, shall continue in effect, subject to their compliance with terms and conditions set forth, until terminated in accordance with the provisions thereof.

In legal terms: Where any Federal lands included within the park by Public Law 81-787 were legally occupied or utilized on September 14, 1950, for residential or grazing purposes, or for other purposes not inconsistent with the act of August 25, 1916, pursuant to a lease, permit, or license issued by the United States, the person so occupying or utilizing such lands, and his heirs, successors, or assigns, shall, upon the termination of such lease, permit, or license, be entitled to have the privileges so possessed or enjoyed by him, renewed from time to time for a period of 25 years from September 14, 1950, and thereafter during the lifetime of such person and the lifetime of his heirs, successors, or assigns, but only if they were .members of his immediate family on such date, provided that grazing privileges appurtenant to privately owned lands located within Grand Teton National Park established by Public Law 81-787 shall not be withdrawn until title to land to which such privileges are appurtenant shall have vested in the United States, except for failure to comply with the applicable regulations.

None of the aforementioned shall apply to any lease, permit, or license for mining purposes or for public accommodations and services, or to any occupancy for utilization of lands for purely temporary purposes.

The Wyoming Game and Fish Commission and the National Park Service shall devise from technical and other information assembled and produced by studies conducted jointly by personnel of the agencies involved, and recommend to the Secretary of the Interior and the Governor of Wyoming for their joint approval, a program to ensure the permanent conservation of elk within Grand Teton National Park. Such programs shall include the controlled reduction of elk in the park by qualified and experienced hunters licensed by the State of Wyoming and deputized as rangers by the Secretary of the Interior, when it is found necessary for the purpose or proper management and protection of the elk. This shall only apply to the park area lying east of the Snake River and those lands west of Jackson Lake and the Snake River that lie north of the 1929 northern park boundary of Grand Teton National Park, but shall not be applicable to lands within the Jackson Hole Wildlife Park. If and when reduction in the number of elk by this method in Grand Teton National Park is required as a part of this program, only one elk may be killed by each licensed deputized ranger.

Other Legislative and Administrative Commitments

By the act of August 9, 1955, the Secretary of the Interior was authorized to construct in Grand Teton National Park, on a location agreed to by the Secretary of the Interior and the Governor of Wyoming, a highway to replace former U.S. Highway 89, also numbered U.S. 187 and U.S. 26. Upon the highway's completion, the Secretary is authorized to enter into an agreement with the State upon such terms and conditions he deems in the interest of the United States for the conveyance of the highway to the State in exchange for State and county roads in the park area.

A memorandum of agreement of May 5, 1955, between the National Park Service and the State of Wyoming, relates to the east side road (U.S. 89, 187, and 26 — also referred to as the Jackson Hole Highway) in Grand Teton National Park. This agreement contains the following stipulation: " . . . Upon completion of the east side highway and subject to the enactment or the necessary enabling legislation, the Government agrees to convey all of its right, title and interest herein to the State of Wyoming." Further: "In consideration of the conveyance to it of the east side highway, the State of Wyoming agrees to convey to the United States of America and its assigns all of the right, title and interest of the State of Wyoming and the County of Teton in and to the State and County roads within the boundaries of Grand Teton National Park or such portions thereof as may be mutally agreed upon at the time the east side highway is conveyed to the State."

A memorandum of understanding dated June 18, 1952, exists between the Department of Interior's National Park Service and the Bureau of Sport Fisheries of the Department of Interior's Fish and Wildlife Service regarding the raising of hay on lands of Grand Teton National Park for the winter feeding of the Jackson Hole elk herd. These lands are located east of Blacktail Butte, south of the north line of secs. 25, 26, 27, 28, and 29, T. 43 N., R. 115 W., 6th PM, north of the Gros Ventre River and west of the eastern park boundary. The National Park Service agrees to make these lands available for this purpose under the terms of this agreement, effective for 20 years beginning July 1, 1952. The agreement has been extended for a 3-year period, after which time the lands involved are to be returned to a natural state.

By a letter dated February 18, 1964, Assistant Secretary of the Interior John A. Carver, Jr., advised that the National Park Service will treat boat traffic on the Snake River within the national park as if the stream were navigable. The administrative decision provides for full emphasis upon safety requirements for waterborne craft, but the management of river float operations is to be limited to the National Park Service jurisdictional authority over the land to the edge of the waterway.

By a memorandum of understanding dated November 29, 1956, between the National Park Service and the Bureau of Reclamation, certain agreements were made concerning Jackson Lake Reservoir, Minidoka Project, in Grand Teton National Park. More specifically, the general areas covered are as follows:

The areas under reclamation withdrawal for Jackson Lake Reservoir, Minidoka Project, fall under the primary jurisdiction of the Bureau of Reclamation, for use or occupancy as it deems necessary for reclamation activities. This does not preclude park development within the operation zone, but does make primary the purpose of operation and protection of the reservoir.

The Bureau of Reclamation retains complete and exclusive control of the flow and utilization of the waters of Jackson Lake Reservoir for reclamation purposes, including the right to raise and lower the reservoir at will. However: "The Bureau will give full consideration to maintaining a constant level of the operating pool, with little or no fluctuation during the recreation season — June through September."

The Jackson Hole Research Station, operated by the University of Wyoming and the New York Zoological Society, is authorized under a special-use permit to conduct research activities in the park until December 31, 1984. The research station, containing approximately 10 acres, is located near the old Moran townsite.

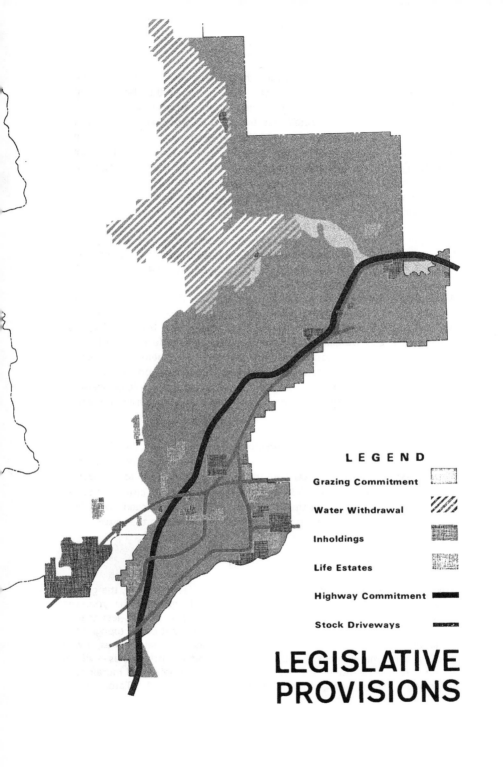

LEGEND

Grazing Commitment

Water Withdrawal

Inholdings

Life Estates

Highway Commitment

Stock Driveways

LEGISLATIVE PROVISIONS

A lease for establishing and operating the Jackson Hole Wildlife Park, near the Snake River's oxbow bend, was a reservation in the deed from the Jackson Hole Preserve, Inc., to the United States on December 16, 1949. A partial surrender of lease dated October 15, 1952, granted to the United States all interest in leased lands, including improvements and personal property thereon, with a stipulation that the United States would continue operation of the wildlife park. In September, 1972, the board of directors of Jackson Hole Preserve, Inc., agreed that the manmade facilities of the wildlife park were no longer desirable, and may be removed, thus eliminating the distinction between this area and the remainder of the park.

A perpetual right of ingress and egress to and from Two Ocean Lake Reservoir is a deed reservation covered in the deed from the Jackson Hole Preserve, Inc., to the United States, dated December 16, 1949.

A memorandum of understanding dated March 31, 1959, between the State of Wyoming's Game and Fish Commission, the U.S. Department of Agriculture's Forest Service, and the U.S. Department of Interior's National Park Service and Bureau of Sport Fisheries and Wildlife of the Fish and Wildlife Service, relates to the maintenance and management of the Jackson Hole elk herd. This agreement sets organization of an advisory council and a technical committee for a program known as the "Jackson Hole Cooperative Elk Studies." There is no established time limit for this memorandum, which became effective July 1, 1958.

Former National Park Service Director Wirth committed the Service to provide certain improvements for the Jackson Hole airport. Included was a runway extension from 6,300 feet to 8,000 feet, designed to adequately handle twin-engine Convair 580's in use by commercial airlines. Former Director Hartzog has stated that the extension will not exceed 1,700 feet, with not more than 300 feet to the north, and 1,400 feet to the south.

THE RESOURCE

Towering 7,000 feet above the sagebrush flats of Jackson Hole, the granite peaks of the Teton Range dominate the park landscape. The youngest mountains of the Rocky Mountain chain, they began to rise less than 9 million years ago. The range, a notable example of fault-block topography, presents a splendid alpine spectacle. Picturesque glacial cirques, living glaciers, awesome canyons, tumbling streams, and beautiful lakes — all are found here. At the mountains' base, dammed by terminal glacial moraines of surprisingly recent times, a series of large lakes mirrors the Tetons' steep slopes and jagged peaks.

The rise of the Teton Range has had a profound influence upon all living things in the region. In the relative coolness of Jackson Hole, a coniferous forest fairly typical of the central and northern Rocky Mountains has developed. The mountain slopes and the lower prominences rising from the floor of the valley are clothed largely in conifers — limber, lodgepole, and whitebark pine; Engelmann spruce; sub-alpine fir; and Douglas-fir. Aspen stands still occur in the upland areas, but many exhibit declining vitality, the result of the area's long-continued protection from fire. Sagebrush dominates the porous, cobbly flatland of the valley floor; but the slopes of morainal ridges and such mountain-peak remnants as Blacktail Butte are wooded, and bands of cottonwood, willow, and spruce line the meandering courses of the Snake River and its tributaries.

An impressive array of wildlife occurs in the park, and can often be easily observed by the public.

Moose frequent the canyons, ponds, and river bottoms at quite predictable times; beaver and muskrat are common in park waters. Sizeable bands of elk appear routinely throughout the visitor season in certain easily accessible areas, and their numbers are greatly augmented by migrating animals in the fall and spring. American pronghorns are often visible on the sagebrush flats east of the Snake River. Bighorn sheep can be seen in the mountains, although this requires considerably more effort. Black bear are often observed in the park's forested areas; their formidable cousin, the grizzly, is occasionally seen, usually in the northern region of the park. Coyotes are frequently observed — and even more commonly heard — throughout the park, as they hunt the numerous rodents and other small vertebrates, and the weak and sick among the larger animals. A small band of bison wanders the lowlands.

Birdlife in the park is varied and often dramatic, although dominated in the public eye by the bald eagle — a few nesting pairs return to the park each year — and by the once nearly extinct trumpeter swan, which now can be easily observed on a number of the park's ponds and streams. Other waterfowl and shore birds are abundant. In the sagebrush flats, the sage grouse may often be seen; in the wooded areas, hikers might encounter grouse along the trails. And the ardent ornithologist can find a great many of the less spectacular, although no less appealing, birds that abound in the park's varied habitats.

Notable among the stream-course faunal systems are those found in and along the Snake River. Here is one of the last remaining natural habitats for the Snake River cutthroat trout. The river is also home to the mountain whitefish. Introduced rainbow, eastern brook, and lake trout inhabit some of the lakes and small streams, as well as portions of the Snake River.

For the perceptive eye, a host of smaller mammals, birds, reptiles, and insects interact in a complex web necessary to sustain the entire ecosystem. It is on this scale — totally unfamiliar to the casual visitor — that the secrets of adaptation and evolution in response to this harsh environment can be most clearly illustrated to the visitor.

The resources of Grand Teton National Park — the geologic wonders, the appeal of the plant and animal inhabitants, the magnetic appeal of the rocky mountain faces — have values to humanity far exceeding that of their sheer physical existence or their provision of a setting for recreation.

The recentness of the area's diastrophic geological activities, and the ease with which their effects can be viewed, are probably no more significant than is the feel of cold rock surfaces against a mountaineer's fingertips or the heart-stopping view of a sheer rock face as seen over the shoulder of a struggling climber.

The perfection of Grand Teton National Park's alpine beauties is meaningless except as it affects the human psyche — whether that of the drive-through traveler viewing the range from U.S. 26, or that of the trail rider bathed in the alpenglow that radiates from the faces of the peaks above the evening gloom of Cascade Canyon.

The characteristics of the plant communities, and even the ecological principles to which they demonstrably respond, may mean less in the long run than does the impact of their forms, scents, and textures upon the emotions of hikers, river runners, riders, and overlook-users. In a world increasingly devoid of harmonious contact between man and nature, the visual effect of morning mists rising from a tranquil beaver pond is surely as significant as is the intriguing story of the role of beavers in shaping and responding to their environment.

Although the park's wildlife is of considerable scientific interest, and is worthy of protection on its own merit, to most park visitors its real significance lies in the excitement they feel when spotting a band of elk drifting out from Timbered Island on a summer evening, hearing the indescribable sound of elk bugling on a crisp fall day, accepting the risk of face-to-face confrontation with bears in the backcountry, or watching a coyote stalk the ground squirrels so abundant on the sagebrush flats. Possession of a trophy lake trout may be considerably less significant than the opportunity to see a Snake River cutthroat swimming easily in the crystalline water of Blacktail Spring Creek at spawning time; and the bald eagle takes on meaning beyond its symbolic one when seen rising from the water with a fish clutched in its talons.

The incredible beauty of the park's winter scene — that virginal quality wildlands have when buried beneath a deep mantle of snow, and the special kind of silence that pervades such a scene — means at least as much to the quality of human life as do the insulating qualities and moisture content of the snow, or its potential for snowmobiling. Unique resources, yes; but even more important, these are the providers of limitless options for rewarding human experiences.

Although Grand Teton National Park has been designated a natural area and its greatest values are essentially inspirational and ecological, varied recreational activities have long been enjoyed within its boundaries. Hiking, horseback riding, cross-country skiing, mountain climbing, snow planing, fishing, and river floating and boating are all popular pastimes. Power-boating has become established on Jackson, Jenny, and Phelps Lakes.

The area's human history is a significant part of the park experience. European man, although a resident of comparatively recent arrival, has, of course, become an integral part of the scene in Jackson Hole. Buildings and pastures remain as vestiges of an era of ranching that began in 1884, and they present opportunities for interpreting the area's recent human history. Few traces remain of the earlier trappers and explorers, many of whom passed through Jackson Hole en route to annual rendezvous where they sold their catches, obtained supplies, and dissipated in gusty revelry. Tough, taciturn, and often illiterate, these men left few precise accounts of their activities; only a shadowy impression remains. But the story of their way of life holds special fascination for modern visitors.

In addition, archeological discoveries document man's presence within Jackson Hole as early as 9,000 years ago. But the record thus far is disjointed. What were the origins of those first hunters, who probably saw glaciers reaching out onto the floor of Jackson Hole? Did they migrate from great distances? A fascinating story of man coping with a changing environment will undoubtedly be revealed as knowledge accumulates.

LAND STATUS

From the standpoint of management, the park's resources must be considered in terms of the ownership of the lands within — and beyond — park boundaries. The boundary established by Public Law 81-787 encompasses an area of 310,350.18 acres. This acreage, as of November 1, 1972, is broken down as follows:

	Acres
Federal	304,353.47
State School Land	1,405.91
Teton County	11.49
Private	4,579.31

Private tracts within the park number in excess of 160 and involve nearly 128 ownerships. The majority of land adjacent to Grand Teton National Park is owned by the United States and falls under the management of either Targhee National Forest or Teton National Forest. Private land accounts for less than 5 percent of Teton County; this situation results in a great concern about loss of land to tax rolls, and also contributes to escalating land values in real-estate sales. The price range for land at the beginning of 1972 was between $6,000 and $25,000 per acre.

REGIONAL CONSIDERATIONS

Grand Teton National Park, together with Yellowstone National Park, comprises the strategic core of a vast upland wilderness, which is held almost exclusively within Federal ownership. Five national forests and parts of three others define its perimeter. Centered primarily within northwestern Wyoming, astride the Continental Divide, it extends into Montana on the north and into Idaho on the west. This 27,000-square-mile region is slightly larger than Vermont, New Hampshire, Massachusetts, and Rhode Island, combined.

By any standard, this region rivals Alaska in its wilderness qualities and its variety and number of large mammals. As impressive as its scenic wonders is its history — in essence a spectrum of the Nation's westward expansion, including as it does exploration, trapping, Indian wars, mining, railroads, logging, ranching, and homesteading.

Carved out of the public domain between 1872 and 1907, primarily to prevent over-exploitation of a critical watershed, this area, through Federal management, served to stabilize an emerging agriculture-based economy. Government sponsorship under the Reclamation Act of 1902 led to the construction of reservoirs and diversion canals on the peripheral lands to store and distribute the snowmelt from the mountain uplands, and this

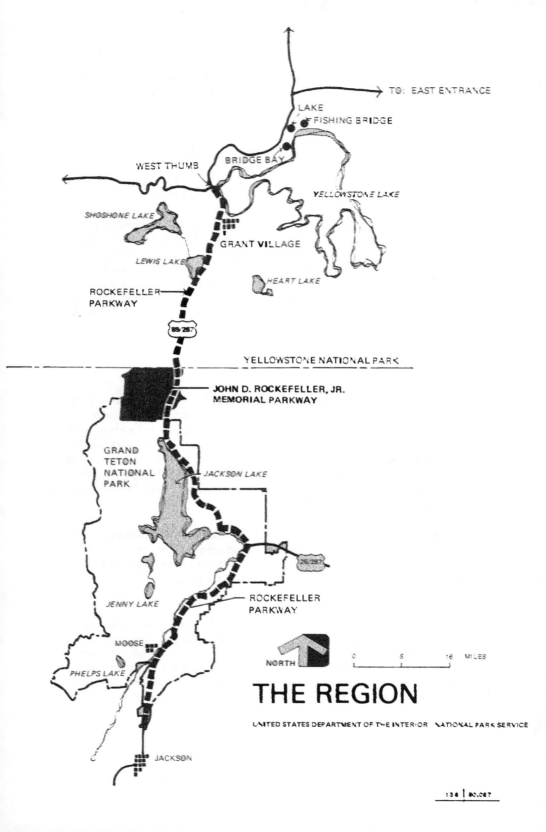

TO: EAST ENTRANCE

LAKE
FISHING BRIDGE

BRIDGE BAY

WEST THUMB

YELLOWSTONE LAKE

SHOSHONE LAKE

GRANT VILLAGE

LEWIS LAKE

HEART LAKE

ROCKEFELLER
PARKWAY

85/287

YELLOWSTONE NATIONAL PARK

JOHN D. ROCKEFELLER, JR.
MEMORIAL PARKWAY

GRAND
TETON
NATIONAL
PARK

JACKSON LAKE

26/28

JENNY LAKE

ROCKEFELLER
PARKWAY

MOOSE

PHELPS LAKE

NORTH

0   5   16   MILES

THE REGION

UNITED STATES DEPARTMENT OF THE INTERIOR   NATIONAL PARK SERVICE

JACKSON

beyond — park boundaries. The boundary established by Public Law 81-787 encompasses an area of 310,350.18 acres. This acreage, as of November 1, 1972, is broken down as follows:

	Acres
Federal	304,353.47
State School Land	1,405.91
Teton County	11.49
Private	4,579.31

Private tracts within the park number in excess of 160 and involve nearly 128 ownerships. The majority of land adjacent to Grand Teton National Park is owned by the United States and falls under the management of either Targhee National Forest or Teton National Forest. Private land accounts for less than 5 percent of Teton County; this situation results in a great concern about loss of land to tax rolls, and also contributes to escalating land values in real-estate sales. The price range for land at the beginning of 1972 was between $6,000 and $25,000 per acre.

REGIONAL CONSIDERATIONS

Grand Teton National Park, together with Yellowstone National Park, comprises the strategic core of a vast upland wilderness, which is held almost exclusively within Federal ownership. Five national forests and parts of three others define its perimeter. Centered primarily within northwestern Wyoming, astride the Continental Divide, it extends into Montana on the north and into Idaho on the west. This 27,000-square-mile region is slightly larger than Vermont, New Hampshire, Massachusetts, and Rhode Island, combined.

By any standard, this region rivals Alaska in its wilderness qualities and its variety and number of large mammals. As impressive as its scenic wonders is its history — in essence a spectrum of the Nation's westward expansion, including as it does exploration, trapping, Indian wars, mining, railroads, logging, ranching, and homesteading.

Carved out of the public domain between 1872 and 1907, primarily to prevent over-exploitation of a critical watershed, this area, through Federal management, served to stabilize an emerging agriculture-based economy. Government sponsorship under the Reclamation Act of 1902 led to the construction of reservoirs and diversion canals on the peripheral lands to store and distribute the snowmelt from the mountain uplands, and this

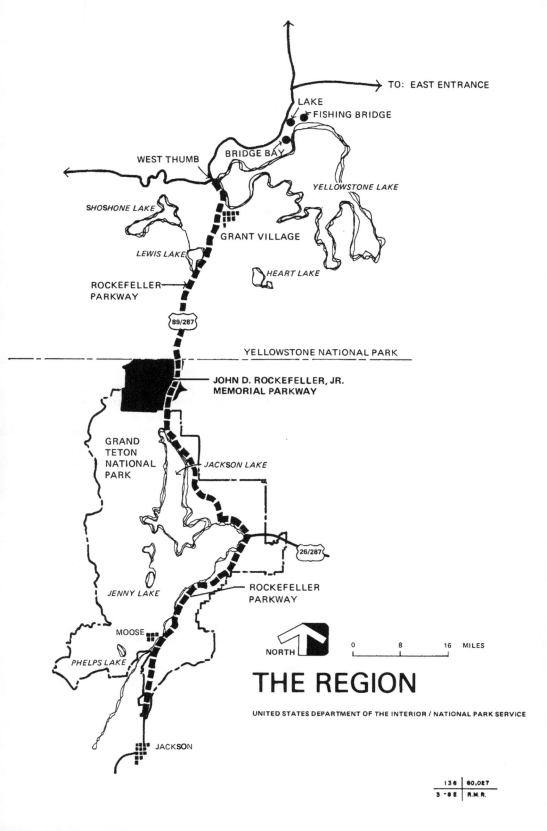

TO: EAST ENTRANCE

LAKE
FISHING BRIDGE

WEST THUMB

BRIDGE BAY

YELLOWSTONE LAKE

SHOSHONE LAKE

GRANT VILLAGE

LEWIS LAKE

HEART LAKE

ROCKEFELLER
PARKWAY

89/287

YELLOWSTONE NATIONAL PARK

JOHN D. ROCKEFELLER, JR.
MEMORIAL PARKWAY

GRAND
TETON
NATIONAL
PARK

JACKSON LAKE

26/287

JENNY LAKE

ROCKEFELLER
PARKWAY

MOOSE

PHELPS LAKE

NORTH

0   8   16   MILES

THE REGION

UNITED STATES DEPARTMENT OF THE INTERIOR / NATIONAL PARK SERVICE

JACKSON

136	80,027
3 -82	R.M.R.

construction further entrenched and expanded the agricultural base of the surrounding basin lands. Urban shift following World War II eroded this stability, however.

Today, providing opportunities for outstanding outdoor experiences dominates the region's economy. Although summer use has predominated, the increasing popularity of winter activities is leading to a stable year-round tourist economy. Vying for the skiier's dollar are Teton Village and Snow King, in Jackson Hole; and Grand Targhee, a few miles away on the west side of the Tetons. West Yellowstone is emerging as a center for snowmobiling at the region's western portal.

Realistically: If the increase in public interest in such activities is to be responded to without destruction of the unique assets upon which this growth is based, relevant regional and local planning and subsequent zoning must be established and vigorously acted upon. Likewise, limited developable land (less than 5 percent of Teton County is privately owned), critical wildlife ranges, and historically established watershed responsibilities suggest a need for guidelines and zoning for even the limited residual grazing, lumbering, and mining that continues in the region.

An overall plan for preserving the region's prime scenic attributes must be developed; likewise, guidelines for the management of rare and endangered species have to be established and enforced. Also, an integrated solid-waste-disposal plan needs to be devised for the region. It is in this area of concern that the most substantial steps already have been taken, through a multi-agency regional landfill operation. Finally, a comprehensive regional transportation plan must be developed. Critical to this requirement is the need to develop all-weather intra-regional ground transportation. And certainly, consideration of alternatives to the core parks' already-overloaded road systems is warranted.

Since the ultimate resolution of all these issues will have an important bearing on the long-range plans of all the entities involved, efforts to upgrade the coordination of planning for land and water resources within the region should be expanded. Only within such a framework can the region's unique qualities be preserved.

Because of its responsibilities in the core parks, the National Park Service must play a key role in the development and implementation of plans, based on regional considerations, to make rational responses to the public's needs. This principle underlies the discussions and proposals in the following master plan for Grand Teton National Park.

the plan

A sound system of evaluation and classification of lands and waters in a national park is a prerequisite for master planning. The National Park Service's land classification system gives recognition and protection to park resources, and provides for varied types and levels of visitor use within each classification. This system directs and controls day-to-day management of these important resources, and provides the framework for the concepts upon which this master plan is based.

LAND CLASSIFICATION

Class I: High-Density Recreation
Two areas, Colter Bay and Jackson Lake Lodge, are classified in this category. Readily accessible both to the park's primary transportation corridor and Jackson Lake, they offer a large variety of visitor accommodations and services, which include diverse lodging facilities, a swimming pool, horse concessions, food, and automotive services.

Class II: General Outdoor Recreation
Park roads, campgrounds, low-density lodging, low-density concessioner services, and residential and operation enclaves are placed in this category. Although these areas will be managed to provide for visitor needs, preservation of the natural setting should be considered.

Class III: Natural Environment
This classification encompasses the valley lands committed to special uses as defined by legislation, such as grazing, stock driveways, and life estates. Visitor facilities permitted within these lands include bicycle trails, informal picnic sites, and primitive camping areas. The park's Class III lands serve primarily as a buffer or transition zone, with low-density use that has little impact on the ecological processes. Collectively, they provide the setting for the park's Class IV lands; and as such, their value is comparable to that of the Class IV areas themselves. Some Class III lands eventually should be considered for Class IV or V designation when adverse uses can be eliminated.

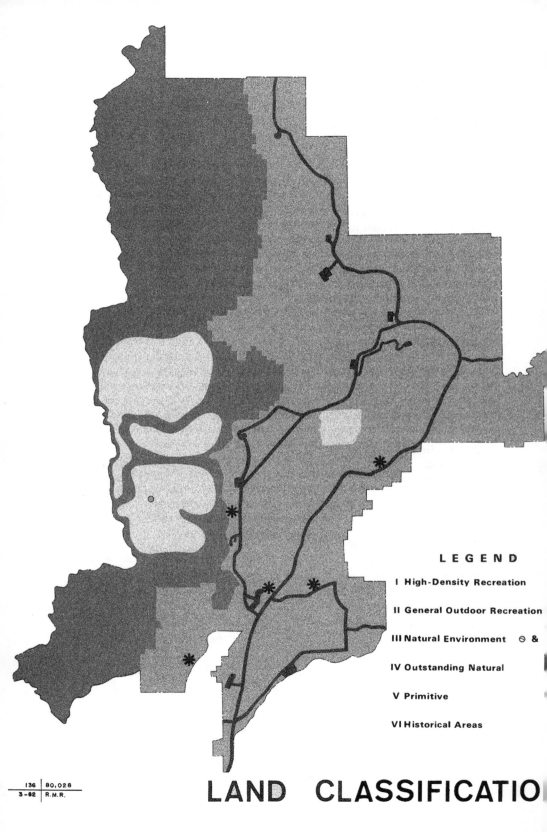

LEGEND

I High-Density Recreation

II General Outdoor Recreation

III Natural Environment ⊖ &

IV Outstanding Natural

V Primitive

VI Historical Areas

136 | 80,028
3-82 | R.M.R.

LAND CLASSIFICATIO

Class IV: Outstanding Natural
In Grand Teton, these areas comprise the most spectacular sections of the Teton Range, and the outstanding section of the Potholes. The Class IV sections of the mountains are of primary interest and comprise the principal rationale for the establishment of the park; the Potholes area is outstanding geologically, and is a crucial element of the scenic foreground of the range. The highest priority will be given to the protection of these areas.

No development, or proliferation, of the present trail system will be permitted. Visitors may travel into these areas, and may stay overnight, but no campsite preparation, tree or vegetation removal, or wood fires will be permitted. Upon termination of existing grazing rights, the outstanding portions of the Potholes area will be managed as Class IV lands.

Class V: Primitive
These spectacular, undeveloped lands with no roads provide the principal wildland setting for the Class IV areas. Because their management will be directed toward the preservation of backcountry experiences, no permanent shelters or developed campsites will be permitted. No mechanized vehicles, except those authorized for emergency service, will be allowed.

Class VI: Historical
Remains of prehistoric settlement and historic utilization by modern man are both present. These will be featured as significant parts of the park interpretive story.

VISITOR USE

The pattern of use that past development and the shape of the land have engendered is essentially one of varying levels of involvement, moving from the typical drive-through experience on the sagebrush flats in the east, through the day-use activities on the flats and moraine west of the Snake River, to the relatively strenuous experiences offered by the less accessible mountain peaks in the west. This pattern of use makes basically good sense; however, specific modifications, refinements, and ultimately some reorganization will be required if the park is to make the best use of its resources.

Critical to such a re-tuning is the Service's recognition of the fact that not all visitors seek the same experience or degree of involvement with the park's resources. Many can achieve satisfaction simply from viewing scenery from

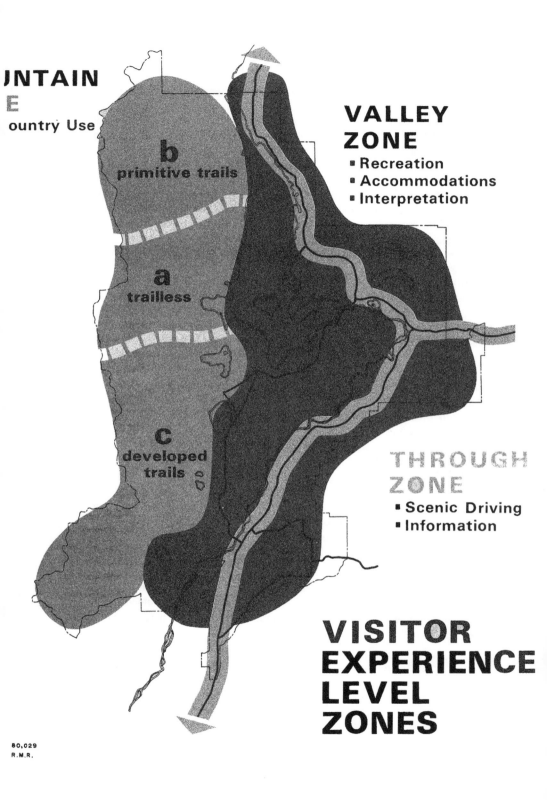

JNTAIN
E
ountry Use

b
primitive trails

a
trailless

c
developed
trails

**VALLEY
ZONE**
▪ Recreation
▪ Accommodations
▪ Interpretation

**THROUGH
ZONE**
▪ Scenic Driving
▪ Information

**VISITOR
EXPERIENCE
LEVEL
ZONES**

80,029
R.M.R.

their automobiles, some can only find fulfillment within the context of the social framework of group activities appropriate to a natural area, while others seek the wilderness solitude that only a trail-less backcountry can provide. Such a range of alternatives carried on within defined zones is not only valid from the visitors' standpoint but is also valid from a management standpoint, because it facilitates the determination of tolerable levels of use in each zone and allows the manager to apply appropriate development and management techniques to provide for particular uses. Following is a description of these zones — Through, Valley, and Mountain — and a discussion of methods for reinforcing specific elements of use in each:

The Through-Zone
This zone is a corridor embracing the through-highways bisecting the Valley Zone.

Although considered an intrusion by some, this through-route, actually a segment of U.S. Routes 89, 187, 26, and 287, has provided a scenic drive-through experience — with a very low per-person impact upon prime park resources — for those not inclined or able to allot sufficient time to appreciate the interior park.

In addition to receiving the interpretive information obtainable at existing overlooks, visitors in this zone may be informed of the range of activities and facilities available within the other park zones, and of the necessity for restraint in their use.

The Valley Zone
Broadly defined, this zone encompasses all the land within the park east of the Teton Range, excluding the through-highway corridor. This is primarily Class III land, and extremely important as the mountain foreground. Because of the varied character of the resources encompassed, it offers considerable diversity in opportunities for day-use activities and for the less strenuous forms of longer term experiences. The great majority of the park's campsites lie in this section, and interpretive activities and facilities are centered here. Within this zone are the man-altered expanses of Jackson Lake, which offer fishing and boating opportunities more commonly associated with recreation areas, and the winding course of the Snake River, which invites tens of thousands of visitors each year to drift down its wild, relatively unspoiled reaches on motorless craft. Yet it also embraces extensive areas of high potential value as outstanding national and/or wilderness lands. The Valley Zone acts as both buffer and springboard to the more fragile backcountry that dominates it. When visitors enter this zone, they gain opportunities to interact more intimately with the resource — to get out and get involved.

19

They must be encouraged to leave their cars if this personal involvement is to be realized, for the intention is that most of their time in the area will be spent without dependence upon automobiles. As many alternatives as feasible, without injury to the resources, should be offered visitors to see and acquire a feeling for the area. Traditional activities will be featured: float trips, boating, fishing, horseback riding, hiking, and bicycling, in summer; ski-touring, snowshoeing, ice-fishing, appropriate oversnow vehicle travel, in winter; and interpretive events and special tours in all seasons.

Because this area's resources inevitably receive the heaviest impact, major efforts must be made to keep resource damage to a minimum. Particular care must be taken with respect to the provision of facilities in this zone, because sizeable parts of it should be considered for re-classification when nonconforming uses are terminated. Particularly careful thought must be given to future treatment of the Jackson Hole airport, because it intrudes directly upon Class III mountain-foreground land, and its air traffic profoundly influences virtually all of the park and its visitors.

The existing interior road superimposes a conflicting through-experience upon an already high-density activity zone, resulting in congestion during peak summer use periods. Some form of supplemental interpretive and transportation system, serving and connecting the park's visitor-service and interpretive hubs, must be devised for this zone, leading toward the eventual elimination of visitor dependence upon private motor vehicles for access to, and enjoyment of, the area. At this time, it is difficult to state what type of system or vehicles will be used, since cost, public acceptance, and availability of equipment will influence the decision. As an interim step, the Jenny Lake road will be maintained as a one-way road, and improved bus service will be provided. In any event, no action will be taken unless it favorably affects the experiences available to park visitors and the protection of park resources.

The residential and service facilities at Beaver Creek, Taggart Creek, and Jenny Lake are to be phased out as soon as alternative facilities can be provided in less significant areas. Stringent pollution controls will be instituted to further reduce any negative environmental impact that the existing and replacement facilities might have.

The Mountain Zone
This zone encompasses all of the Teton Range lying within the park. Much of its area is Class V, embracing the Class IV focal points of the park; the single-acre enclave is Class III. Each of its three sub-units offers distinctive opportunities for the visitor, governed by the density of use to which trail development — or non-development — lends itself. The three sub-units and

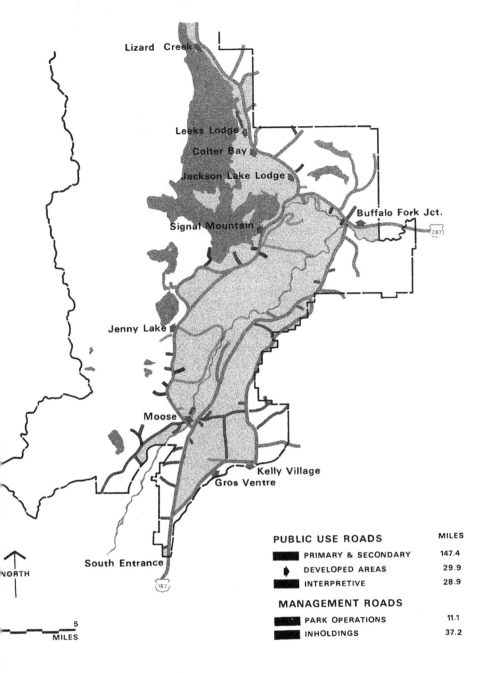

Lizard Creek

Leeks Lodge

Colter Bay

Jackson Lake Lodge

Signal Mountain

Buffalo Fork Jct.

287

Jenny Lake

Moose

Kelly Village

Gros Ventre

South Entrance

187

NORTH

5
MILES

PUBLIC USE ROADS	MILES
PRIMARY & SECONDARY	147.4
DEVELOPED AREAS	29.9
INTERPRETIVE	28.9

MANAGEMENT ROADS	
PARK OPERATIONS	11.1
INHOLDINGS	37.2

EXISTING CIRCULATION

the general approach to be taken in the management of each are described below:

Sub-Unit A occupies the middle segment of the backcountry, between Leigh Canyon and Webb Canyon, west of the reclamation withdrawal line. In this sub-unit, the visitor mingles with nature essentially on the latter's own terms, without the aid of trails or other permanent improvements. This zone is distinguished by its extraordinary capacity to provide a sense of a direct relationship with the environment, and a sense of total self-reliance. It is essential that human use of this sub-unit be kept at levels low enough to maintain, untarnished, the area's pristine quality. The southern half of this sub-unit is Class IV; the balance, Class V.

Sub-Unit B, the northern backcountry between Webb Canyon and the park boundary, provides an intermediate level of backcountry experience. The relatively primitive trails of this sub-unit will be retained; maintenance should be minimal; no other trails should be added. Although less challenging than Sub-Unit A, and perhaps less spectacular than the remainder of the Mountain Zone, this sub-unit — less accessible than Sub-Unit C — gives a sense of great breadth and wildness. This sub-unit is all Class V land.

Sub-Unit C is the most accessible and encompasses the most spectacular scenery of the park's Mountain Zone. Because it embraces the Teton Range's most challenging peaks, this zone offers what is looked upon by mountaineers as the park's ultimate experience. Much of this area is Class IV, interspersed by some Class V lands. Use of this sub-unit has already reached levels that require the application of management techniques to further reduce and control impact on the resources. Here, as in other parts of the park, visitor use is regulated by limitations imposed upon camping through a designation and reservation system. The success of such control is greatly dependent upon the adequate presence of protection personnel. Although parts of this sub-unit may already have exceeded saturation levels of use, diversion of this pressure to either of the other sub-units by improved access or facilities should not be attempted.

INTERPRETATION AND INFORMATION

To enhance the visitor's experience, regional and park orientation and interpretation must be expanded and tailored to fit the needs of the individual. Park visitors and neighbors should be made keenly aware of the extraordinary opportunities for pleasure and learning to be found in its unique combination of natural and cultural resources.

Ideally, information/contact centers should be placed on the periphery of the region, preferably where intra-regional road corridors intersect principal interstate routes. The States in which these centers are located should operate them. These centers should furnish both State and regional information. The National Park Service would provide exhibits, films, brochures, and similar materials. The chambers of commerce from gateway communities, the Forest Service, and other agencies should participate, so the visitor could be informed of the spectrum of recreation and special events available within the region. An information/contact station of this type is being planned for installation north of Jackson — a joint venture of the Wyoming State Highway Commission, the Forest Service, the Bureau of Sport Fisheries and Wildlife, local groups, and the National Park Service.

Along with the establishment of these key information centers, the frequent radio broadcasts on regional recreational news should be continued. Broadcast media throughout the region should be enlisted to advise travelers of the status of campground space, alternate open areas along their travel routes, and other pertinent data.

Initial direct contact with park information sources will normally occur at the reception facility proposed north of Jackson and at other principal entry points. Here, in addition to information about available facilities, points of interest, and the range of activities the park affords, some form of general interpretation that will give personal meaning to visitors' stays in the park will also be made available.

Beyond the contact station, interpretation will be keyed to the specific visitor-use zones. Communication within the Through-Zone will necessarily be brief and general for the most part, giving the auto-borne visitor a basic introduction to the park's natural and cultural history and experiential opportunities. Programmed interpretation will be greatest in the Valley Zone. Here, various approaches to programs emphasizing visitor participation will be undertaken, integrating more traditional media — waysides, exhibits, films, publications, talks — and including such services as nature walks, environmental-study-area programs, campfire programs, climbing demonstrations, and photography tours. Within the backcountry itself, interpretation will be accomplished by means exerting little or no permanent impact upon the environment. For example, self-guiding devices such as leaflets or portable audio devices may be provided.

In general, interpretation will be developed along broad themes that highlight the park's natural resources and animate its history, weaving natural and human history together with environmental strands. The geologic story, emphasizing the various surface features that illustrate a continuous record, will be offered at scenic pullouts and in the proposed reception facility. In interpreting the natural history — the vegetation patterns, aquatic life, and terrestrial wildlife — stress should be placed upon distinctive aspects of the ecosystems of Jackson Hole, how each would function when free of man's direct influence, and what influence modern man has had upon this scene. To make this interpretation vital to visitors, techniques must be sought that relate these processes and observed changes to contemporary man and his environment.

Of major interest to nearly every visitor is the park's history. The area still exhibits some physical reminders of human activities from past eras. Five distinct chapters of history can be identified: early man, fur trappers, pioneers and settlers, early mountain climbers, and diversely motivated park visitors. In each case, man had to adapt to the harsh surroundings, and, in turn, altered this environment for his successors. Each of these stories calls for specialized methods that impart a feeling of earlier times to the visitor.

Because it is the logical focus for interpreting the history of human habitation within Jackson Hole, the completion of the restoration of the Menor's historic district should be granted the highest priority. There should be no intrusions such as paved roads, parking areas, introduced shrubbery, non-historic buildings, or powerlines. The environmental education potential or similarly man-oriented sites at the Pfeiffer and Owbow Bend National Environmental Study Areas should be capitalized upon to the fullest extent possible, as should that of the Cunningham Cabin.

The National Park Service communicates by its management actions as powerfully as by its interpretive programs. Its concern for environmental quality is revealed through management practices that take the lead in reducing degradation of resources, and that enhance the quality of human experiences afforded by such resources.

RESOURCE MANAGEMENT

Resource management in Grand Teton has evolved from what is basically a preservationist approach, involving some intensely active programs dealing with single components of the natural scene (such as total fire-control efforts), into an ecosystems approach that gives thorough consideration to all of the park's interrelated components.

Limited knowledge of ecological processes, the effects of inadequate area-designation in terms of wildlife ranges, and the animosities that followed the establishment of the park, have all restricted management's efforts to compensate for all past and present adverse uses. Nevertheless, substantial progress has been made. In fact, although the park is not a complete and independent ecological unit, and numerous departures from pristine conditions still exist, the ecological conditions present when early trappers first entered the area have not been irreparably impaired in much of the park. Furthermore, new insights gleaned from recent problem-oriented research within Grand Teton and Yellowstone National Parks suggest that environmentally regulated ecosystems can ultimately be re-established in Grand Teton. For example, preliminary research has suggested that the moose population in Grand Teton, and certain elk and bison populations in Yellowstone, may tend to be self-regulating without the presence of significant predator populations. In the context of increasing knowledge of these factors, park management will continue to work toward the elimination of the need for an elk reduction in the park.

Also critical to the re-establishment of natural conditions within the park is the need to compensate for the many years of efforts to suppress all forest fires. Such efforts, and others intended to avert natural "catastrophes," have led to unnatural forest patterns. Within the limits imposed by the necessity of protecting human lives and property, something approaching the natural fire regime must be restored. Only by doing this can management hope to restore a reasonably natural mosaic of forest stands, with their accompanying array of animal life. Within similar limitations, floods, natural periodic outbreaks of insects, and similar phenomena must be allowed to occur without human intervention.

Restoration of the park's aquatic ecosystems is complicated by the presence of the dam that raised Jackson Lake to its present levels. The dam was built for irrigation purposes nearly 20 years before establishment of the original Grand Teton National Park. Of special concern within this ecosystem is the Snake River cutthroat trout, representing one of the two large natural river populations of this trout left in the world. Virtual stoppage of water discharge during annual inspection periods, coupled with heavy fishing pressure, has disrupted the river's cutthroat population. To ensure the perpetuation of this endangered native species, construction of a long-sought bypass around the dam is critically needed. In the interim, substantial measures aimed at reducing pressures on cutthroat populations are to be taken. Ultimately, the emphasis must shift to quality rather than quantity, by encouraging alternatives such as catch-and-release fishing.

The meteoric rise in backcountry use is such that further refinements of existing controls over the distribution and forms of use must be effected in order to preserve the park's esthetic values. As a major step toward easing the impact within this critical zone, horse use — other than that required for extended trips into the backcountry — is to be relocated along the eastern boundary of the park. Anticipated increases in backcountry use suggest that other restraints, in addition to those already in effect at such areas as Lake Solitude, Amphitheater Lake, Holly Lake, and Marion Lake, must eventually be imposed, and similar restraints extended to other relatively accessible backcountry focal points. These restrictions would include such regulations as requiring that feed be packed in rather than obtained by grazing or browsing; that stock be tethered during prolonged stops and be kept from lakeside meadows, streams, and lakeshores; that heavily used areas be restricted to day use, with no fires permitted; and that less concentrated camping — or none — be permitted in fragile areas.

In more recent years, the presence of the snowmobile has become a characteristic of the winter scene on the flatlands of the park. With the expected increase in other forms of winter use, there must be continuing re-evaluation of snowmobiling and other uses so that management can initiate appropriate actions to assure opportunities for full enjoyment with minimal impairment of the park's distinctive assets.

The relative merits of motorboating on Jenny and Phelps Lakes must be similarly weighed.

RESOURCE USE CAPACITIES

Implicit in all efforts to accommodate visitors within Grand Teton's various use-zones is the fact that upper limits of use do exist, beyond which resource quality and/or the level of visitors' enjoyment diminishes. In several areas within the park, acceptable levels of use appear to have been exceeded.

Since 1950 and 1958, when the park was expanded and developed, visitation has increased by an average of 5 percent a year, and has surpassed 3 million every year since 1969. Although many of this number are enjoying a scenic drive-through experience, it is the enormous growth in the participative activities that most seriously threatens the park's resources and the quality of visitors' experiences. As an example, registered climbing attempts in 1971 increased by 40 percent over 1969. In addition, 135,000 visitors registered for backcountry hikes in 1971, and undoubtedly there were many more who did not register. Float trips on the Snake River have tripled in 5 years. Campground use reaches saturation levels through most of the summer and is extending more into the off-season periods.

26

Winter use of the park is increasing, and will demand fuller consideration in future plans. Such activities as cross-country skiing, ice fishing, and wildlife observation are all becoming more popular in the park.

The increased pressure on all the resources of Grand Teton could damage or ruin the park's delicate and interdependent elements, and thus diminish or destroy the opportunity for continuing the quality of experiences that could be provided by the park. To prevent the development of such a situation, resource carrying capacities must be established. It is important to understand that in defining these resource carrying capacities, two paramount — sometimes conflicting — considerations are the limiting factors.

The first factor — and that most frequently in the public eye — is the mandate to perpetuate the park's ecosystems in their natural state. All the innovative techniques known cannot adequately insulate the more vulnerable features from endlessly increasing numbers of visitors, so ceilings on these numbers must be established. In many instances, resource deterioration correlates directly with visitor use. The ability of the ecosystem to absorb use without degradation must be the controlling factor in establishing use-ceilings. Once such ceilings are imposed, the recovery or condition of the protected area must be monitored.

The second — and equally important — factor is the assurance of quality visitor experiences. While it may be technically possible to devise methods to move large numbers of visitors through the park without increasing their physical impact on natural features, there is surely a point of diminishing returns, beyond which the presence of more people totally negates the character of experience the park was established to provide. The number of people that can interact and still find the experience they seek as individuals will vary immensely between the main circulation system and the backcountry zones. Methods of identifying optimum densities of the many types of visitors are still less precise than are those of measuring visitor impact upon natural resources.

Ultimately, it will be an integration of the behavioral and natural sciences that will guide the development of a reliable formula for park use. In arriving at such a formula, numerical limits must be established that relate to numbers of people, types of use, and duration of stay in a given area. In addition, such limits must be flexible, so that management can respond to unanticipated environmental or esthetic deterioration, and to improved means of providing for use without abuse.

DEVELOPMENT CEILINGS

In the final analysis, there is a limit to the ability of the park to withstand open-ended overnight accommodation of the public. The qualities that make Grand Teton a source of uniquely rewarding experiences will be lost if public use is permitted to the point that park values are seriously impaired or destroyed. Unlimited development means the eventual destruction of the public's opportunities to benefit from the park. Therefore, ceilings have been established to hold overnight facilities at levels not exceeding those obligated by 1971.

To achieve the rehabilitation of the Jenny Lake, Taggart Creek, and Beaver Creek residential areas, other quarters are needed for both permanent and seasonal park personnel who, by necessity, now occupy substandard, intrusive facilities in these areas. In addition, more residential and operational facilities will be required when the park's staffing more nearly approaches a realistic level.

Among the sites to be considered in responding to the needs for more housing and work space is the developed area at Moose. The seriousness of intrusion on the fragile Snake River floodplain and on the adjacent historic Menor's Ferry complex suggest that development at Moose should cease — and perhaps ultimately be reversed. Alternative sites might be any of several areas near the south or east boundary within the park, or outside the park in or near Jackson.

REGIONAL PLANNING: A NEED FOR THE FUTURE

If Grand Teton National Park is to provide properly for use by this and future generations, coordinated planning involving national parks, national forests, other public lands, and the communities within the region will be essential. Visitor demands for recreation, accommodation, and support services must be considered in regional terms, recognizing the varying capacities of each administrative unit to respond to public needs without serious impairment of its resources and their products (whether those products are material or esthetic, or both).

Although resource consumption on a sustained-yield basis is integral to the management of lands administered by the Bureau of Land Management and the Forest Service (in contrast to that of National Park Service lands), the capacity of those lands to meet recreational demands is just as surely limited as is that of the parks. The kinds, levels, and distribution of activities and support facilities appropriate to each unit must be weighed cooperatively, and realistic limits agreed to in each case.

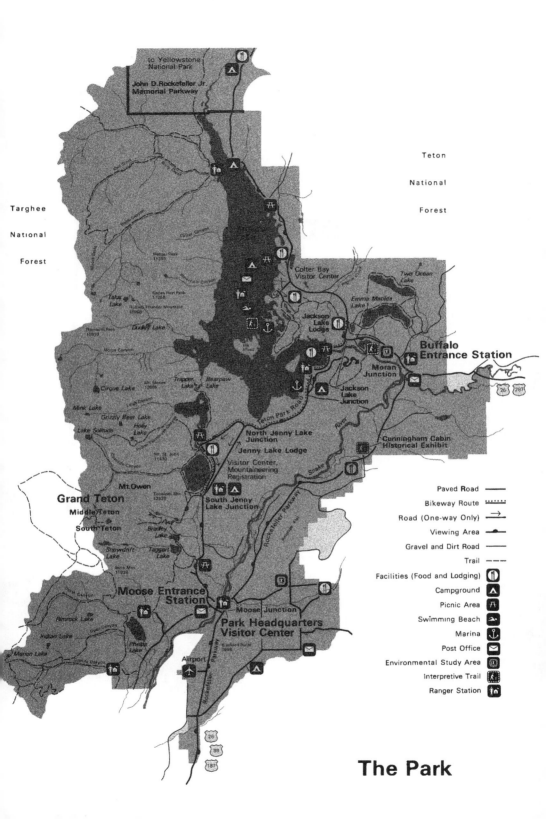

The Park

appendixes

A: MANAGEMENT OBJECTIVES

The following statement by the superintendent of Grand Teton National Park reflects park management's needs and goals relative to this master plan.

General Management

To achieve, through coordination with Federal, State, and local government agencies, in conjunction with private enterprise, a regional cooperative and coordinated program that will perpetuate the natural and historic environmental values, while simultaneously providing for the visitor in a manner that brings appreciation, as well as enlightenment.

To manage Grand Teton National Park in a manner that will focus the attention of the visitor upon seeing, feeling, and understanding the park as a total environmental resource.

To manage Grand Teton National Park on a year-round basis, recognizing the growing interest of the public in its remarkable winter-use opportunities, and in opportunities offered during the "quiet" periods of spring and fall.

To manage the park in such a manner as to relieve the pressures exerted on prime park lands by relocating intrusive residential and operational facilities. The park will continue to be divided into two districts, and functional responsibilities for management of the northern section of the park will be continued from the operating centers at Colter Bay.

To eliminate seasonal National Park Service and concessioner quarters from outlying areas of the park, except where such quarters are essential for security reasons.

To avoid pollution emissions that would degrade the environment.

To provide sewage-treatment facilities to prevent the discharge of any effluent directly into streams or lakes, as well as to avoid the disruption of the area's ecosystems through the pollution or alteration of ground water.

To enhance the natural qualities of water habitats by seeking to give a "lake" rather than a "reservoir" aspect to Jackson Lake, to the extent that it is possible to do so without causing serious impairment to downstream resources. As steps toward this objective, the National Park Service will seek:

> To provide for an agreement with the Bureau of Reclamation to ensure maintenance of Jackson Lake at or very near its full pool elevation of 6,770 feet during the visitor impact period, but only if this can be achieved without sacrificing significant natural values elsewhere.

To develop procedures in cooperation with the Bureau of Reclamation in the operation of Jackson Lake Dam to ensure water flows on the Snake River sufficient to provide adequate aquatic environment for the native fishes, and protection of resources downstream through installation of a bypass facility.

To develop means of transportation that will relieve motor vehicle impact on the Jenny Lake/String Lake areas, and to reduce or eliminate unnecessarily intrusive modes of access elsewhere in the park.

Resource Management
To manage the biotic resources of the park for the purpose of perpetuating the indigenous plant and animal associations of the Teton Range and Jackson Hole, in a condition of as nearly natural dynamic equilibrium as is feasible.

To consider as high priority in all management decisions the scenic quality of the forest mantle lying on the slopes of the Teton Range and facing Jackson Hole, all of which forms an integral part of the scenic resource of mountains and valley.

To manage the Teton Range and selected sections of the lowland areas of the park for their wilderness values.

To develop elk management programs with the Wyoming Game and Fish Commission and the U.S. Department of Agriculture's Forest Service and Bureau of Sport Fisheries and Wildlife, aimed at ultimately eliminating the necessity for a public elk-reduction program on lands within Grand Teton National Park.

To display wildlife under conditions that are natural and unrestrained.

To manage the native Snake River cutthroat trout so as to ensure the perpetuation of a native wild population as part of a natural ecosystem within its range in Grand Teton National Park.

Visitor Use
To hold overnight accommodations to the level that can be managed without increasing the aggregate amount of land now being utilized for visitor services. (The currently approved pillow count is 2,850.) Cooperate with private enterprise and other public agencies in arranging for proper distribution of uses and accommodations within and beyond park boundaries.

To maintain campground capacities at the number currently developed at five locations within the park.

To study existing use and determine carrying capacity; and to determine essential sanitation requirements for designated backcountry campsites.

To study the use-patterns and concessioner services at the Jenny Lake complex, and to reduce visitor impact and environmental damage.

To retain the designated and marked small boat-in campsites of specified carrying capacity on the shores of Jackson and Leigh Lakes for camping and picnic use.

To manage access points to the Snake River for scenic and fishing float trips, so as to perpetuate a natural and wilderness-type environment through which float-trip groups can travel. Undertake studies to determine the capacity of visitor use on and along the Snake River.

To direct trail development and management toward alleviating conflicts between hikers and horseback riders.

To relocate saddle-horse stable areas from the base of the Teton Range to eastern zones of the park. Horse operations along the Mountain Zone of the park will be confined to departure facilities without holding corrals.

To confine dude-ranch operations (a historic activity indigenous to Jackson Hole) within the park to the areas east of the Snake River and along the eastern boundary of the park.

To provide day-use facilities, sanitation, and access points for winter activities in suitable areas of the park.

Interpretation
To increase environmental awareness through an interpretation program stressing the relevance of the resources of the Tetons and Jackson Hole to modern man. The challenge of the mountains and the floral and faunal ecology are key elements in developing this theme.

To interpret the historical resources within the park, not only by giving attention to man's historic niche in this environment, but by interpreting the historical events that took place at Cunningham Cabin, Menor's Ferry, and Maude Noble Cabin, in context with the Nation's history in general. Living-history possibilities are to be considered in the park's interpretive program.

To sharpen public perception of the opportunities for esthetic gratification represented by the unique resources of Grand Teton National Park.

To work with such programs as National Environment Education Development (NEED) to bring a new awareness to the people of the park and its environment.

C: MASTER PLAN ADVISORY TEAM

Chester C. Brown / Chairman, Chief of the Division of International Affairs, National Park Service

Nels Murdock / Former Associate Regional Director (retired), Midwest Region, National Park Service

R. Merrick Smith / Park Planner, Western Service Center, National Park Service

John S. McLaughlin / Superintendent, Sequoia and Kings Canyon National Parks

Jack K. Anderson / Superintendent, Yellowstone National Park

Howard H. Chapman / Superintendent, Grand Teton National Park

Sigurd R. Olson / Consultant, National Park Service

Harold P. Fabian / Consultant

Joe I. Penfold / Conservation Director, Izaak Walton League of America

Daniel A. Poole / President, Wildlife Management Institute

DATE DUE

Demco, Inc. 38-293

Publication services were provided by the graphics and editorial staffs of the Denver Service Center, 1973.

United States Department of the Interior / National Park Service

CPSIA information can be obtained
at www.ICGtesting.com
Printed in the USA
BVHW04*1133200818
525056BV00010B/238/P